D1456429

SHOTS &
SHOOTERS

50 drinks to make a great party

DOG 'n' BONE

Michael Butt

*For Henry Joshua James,
when he is old enough,
and my brother, David Butt,
for everything*

Published in 2014 by Dog 'n' Bone Books
an imprint of Ryland Peters & Small Ltd
519 Broadway, 5th floor, New York NY 10012
20–21 Jockey's Fields, London WC1R 4BW

www.rylandpeters.com

10 9 8 7 6 5 4 3 2 1

A CIP catalog record for this book is available
from the Library of Congress and the
British Library.

ISBN: 978 1 909313 42 2

Printed in China

Designer: Alison Fenton
Design concept: Luis Peral Aranda
Copyeditor: Helen Ridge
Photographer: Martin Norris

Contents

Introduction

"We wanna be free! We wanna be free to do what we wanna do.
And we wanna get loaded. And we wanna have a good time. And
that's what we're gonna do... We're gonna have a good time.
We're gonna have a party."

The Wild Angels (and Primal Scream)

Try remembering your very best nights drinking with friends,
search back through the pain of the recollection of the morning
after, and try to list what you had to drink. I bet that shots
were involved. No other style of drink ensures the clinking of
glasses and the meeting of eyes and minds more than a round
of shots. They encourage you to savor fellowship, to cross the
boundaries of social constraints, and to truly laugh or cry with
the people most important to you.

They don't even have to taste nice; the overcoming of a
challenging or even slightly unpleasant experience together
is what brings everybody closer. If they do taste nice, that
is merely a bonus.

This book is designed to help you make some of the nicest
shots and shooters, and also show you how to enjoy neat liquor
with friends. The recipes are easy and guaranteed to make your
party one of those great, memorable evenings.

So Cheers, Prost, Santé, and Bottoms Up!

Definitions

To make this book easier to use, I have split the drinks into three different types, explained below. Although there are exceptions, generally the "danger levels" read from highest to lowest.

SHOTS

Drinks designed to be consumed in one, consisting of only spirituous ingredients. Normally 1–1½oz (30–45ml).

SHOOTERS

Drinks designed to be consumed in one, consisting of both spirit and nonalcoholic ingredients. Normally 2oz (60ml).

SHORTS

Spirits consumed without a mixer, sipped and savored. Normally 2oz (60ml).

HANGOVER

A catchall definition of a selection of maladies, including, but not limited to, nausea, extreme dehydration, shakes and shivers, banging headaches, and embarrassing memories. Generally caused by overconsumption of shorts, shots, and shooters. DRINK RESPONSIBLY. Alcohol is a social lubricant, not a competition!

Equipment

The drinks in this book are generally pretty easy to make, but there are a few things you will need to have before you start.

Shot Glasses

Although not absolutely necessary (dentist's chair anyone?), shot glasses obviously make the job loads easier and less messy. They come in a huge range of shapes and styles. The most useful is a 2oz (60ml) straight-sided glass, which you can use for most drinks. There is no need to buy specific glasses, but if you are planning to make "bomb" drinks, it is worth getting some tempered single 1oz (30ml) glasses and some strong rocks glasses for the bombs to drop into.

Cocktail Shaker

This doesn't need to be fancy, but if you want to make good shooters, you will need a shaker to mix and chill the ingredients. A preserving jar or Tupperware container will do at a pinch, with a slotted spoon for straining, but the best parties are ones where a little bit of time has been spent on prep, and a proper shaker will make the whole thing loads easier.

Don't Forget Ice!

If you are making shooters, you will need lots. It also comes in handy for mixed drinks, cocktails, and chilling beer!

Bar Spoons

Bar spoons are very useful for floating ingredients, to produce layered shots. They have a circular disc on the handle end of the spoon and a twisted shaft for liquids to pour down. You can easily use a teaspoon instead but you will have to take extra care to get clean divisions between the layers. (See page 16 for floating techniques.)

Basic Ingredients

There are two ways to use this book. The first is to check your liquor cabinet and choose recipes that correspond to the ingredients you already have. The second is to choose recipes you like the look of and purchase the necessary ingredients. Neither way should cause you to have to spend too much money, and party guests will often be happy to bring along a bottle of liquor that you have requested as opposed to wine, flowers, or unwanted chocolates. However, if you are in the habit of entertaining, it is worth stocking up on a few key products to get the party started.

Vodka

Don't break the bank on a douche-friendly super premium bottle. A good Russian, Polish, or Scandinavian vodka will be perfect for all the recipes. Generally, Russian vodka has a bit more heat and spice, which makes it a natural choice for shots.

Tequila

If it says 100% agave on the bottle, it will be fine. Most of the recipes work best with a blanco (silver) tequila but if you have a favorite reposado, that will also work.

Orange Liqueur

A mainstay of the classic cocktailian's liquor cabinet, orange liqueurs are also popular in shots. So much so, it is probably worth having a couple of different ones. Grand Marnier is the key ingredient in a B-52, making it almost a necessity (the drink will still work with Cointreau, though), and to maximize visual effect, a bottle of blue curaçao is a good purchase.

Cream Liqueur

Baileys, or another cream liqueur, is an ingredient in loads of layered shots. It has a very smooth character and is not too strong. Despite being very sweet, the cream ensures that it will float on most liqueurs. It is a store cupboard must-have!

Overproof Spirit

Fire is fun! Flaming drinks are always popular, and if you are careful, perfectly safe. An ingredient at over 100 proof (50% ABV) will help with the process; an overproof white rum, green Chartreuse, or absinthe will all work well. As these are only used in small quantities, half bottles or miniatures can be a sensible purchase.

SHORTS

Every country with a tradition of making alcohol has rituals that have developed alongside the product to encourage celebratory drinking. Every cultural subset has adapted these recipes and created new ones, all in the name of sharing the drinking experience. One of the joys of experimenting with alcohol is working out your favorite style of drink but the choice is often bewildering. This chapter will help you to avoid the pitfalls and find a tipple that really fits.

WHISK(E)Y

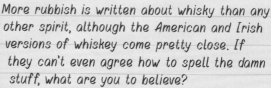

More rubbish is written about whisky than any other spirit, although the American and Irish versions of whiskey come pretty close. If they can't even agree how to spell the damn stuff, what are you to believe?

Some whiskies are scary. The salty, smoky malt whiskies (don't call them Scotch in Scotland unless you want a pummeling) are probably not the best place to start but they can make a satisfying destination. Much easier departure points are Irish, American, and blended whiskies.

When serving any whisk(e)y, the purists will be very specific: malt whisky should be drunk neat or with a dash of water but NEVER ice; American whiskey is often recommended on the rocks. Both ways have their merits, but I think the best way is to dilute to your chosen level and keep cold not with ice, but with actual rocks. Whisky stones are kept in the freezer and chill your whisky without extra dilution: the perfect compromise.

Vodka

Vodka is the world's most widely consumed spirit, with 60 shots downed every second. It is often seen as the easiest way to add alcohol to a mixed drink and that the flavor itself is secondary. This is often true for cocktails, but this book is about drinking spirits on their own, in this case vodka, where the character of the different types really needs to shine through.

To enjoy vodka at its most traditional, and best, it must be chilled. Get your bottle into the freezer at least two hours before serving, and if you have space between the frozen peas and all the ice cream, put the glassware in there as well. Just about any shot glass will suffice but for the most authenticity and fun, try and find some glasses without bases. These ensure that you can't put them down and must finish the shot in one go.

There are loads of very neutral domestic vodkas on the market, made from maize or sugar cane, but when drinking vodka neat, try to get a more characterful brand. Russian vodkas are generally made from wheat and have a good deal of heat on the finish; Polish vodka made from rye has a spicy aroma and taste, while their potato vodka has a very creamy texture. Most Scandinavian and Eastern European vodkas will pair nicely with the traditional foods of the region. They have the ability to cut through smoked meat, oily fish, and creamy dishes, while still being light enough to be enjoyed with shellfish. A Scandinavian crayfish party is a once in a lifetime experience, when everybody must do a shot of vodka every time they eat a crayfish claw, and that is all there is to eat!

BRANDY

Brandy is any spirit distilled from fruit but, confusingly, most of the things with brandy on the label, like apricot brandy, are actually liqueurs, made of neutral spirit and flavored with fruit. Most of the world's brandies masquerade under individual appellations to confuse you, with even grappa and marc considered brandies, despite being made from pits and sticks and leftover skins. For most people, brandy begins and ends with cognac, the most famous grape brandy from Cognac in northeast France.

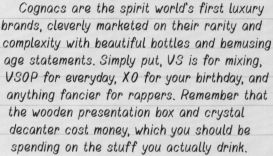

Cognacs are the spirit world's first luxury brands, cleverly marketed on their rarity and complexity with beautiful bottles and bemusing age statements. Simply put, VS is for mixing, VSOP for everyday, XO for your birthday, and anything fancier for rappers. Remember that the wooden presentation box and crystal decanter cost money, which you should be spending on the stuff you actually drink.

Once you have chosen your brand and level of expenditure, the next thing is to throw away any huge brandy snifters, often called balloons, and affectations like candle heaters and the like. One of the joys of cognac, and the reason why it is so expensive, is the huge level of complexity and power of the aroma. Balloons are designed to hold in this aroma, so you can appreciate it, but the fact is they hold so much gaseous ethanol from evaporation that one sniff will knock out your sense of smell for ten minutes. The correct glassware is a small tulip glass, gently warmed in the palm of the hand. These glasses are easily available and have the added bonus of being much cheaper than snifters.

TEQUILA

Tequila is the most misunderstood of beverages, with people often imputing semimystical properties to it, along with an unrivaled capacity to get people ruinously drunk. Only one of these is true and even that isn't tequila's fault.

Tequila is the distilled product of the agave, a succulent plant that grows all over Central America. The agave takes up to eight years to mature before it is harvested by hand and undergoes several processes prior to distillation. This makes tequila expensive to produce, which led to the invention of a cheaper category: mixto tequila. Seemingly made from 51% agave-based alcohol and 49% burnt tires, mixto tequila is NOT worth bothering with and is the gut-rot responsible for all of those teenage hangovers from hell.

The ritual of the salt and lemon or lime was designed to disguise the taste of cheap mixto tequila and has no place in the real drinker's arsenal. Much better is the authentic pairing with Sangrita (see page 54). This savory sidekick, made from orange, spice, and pomegranate, can be sipped or shot alongside a 100% agave tequila.

There are over 600 different tequilas available, and due to the very individual nature of the production process, the amount of residual character from the agave, and the climate where the tequila is aged, they are all very different. To truly appreciate tequila neat, it is worth trying it in a champagne flute or a narrow wine glass, which will allow you to swirl the spirit, to waken it, without the danger of inhaling too much ethanol vapor.

GIN

More has been written on the Martini than any other cocktail. If it were a movie star, it would be Samuel L. Jackson, not for the Ezekiel 25:17 monologue, but for its almost boring cultural ubiquity. It gets everywhere! On every neon sign of every bar, most of which couldn't stir a good Martini if on the receiving end of the aforementioned speech, the olive-packing cocktail glass winks suggestively, but why?

The first reason is clever bartenders understand the value of a drink that requires a degree of personalization; it ensures they talk to the customer enough to get a tip. The second reason is that cold, slightly diluted gin, with a nice salty olive, is damn tasty and pretty much the quickest way to consume hard liquor elegantly.

Pedants may argue that this isn't a neat spirit, because the pesky vermouth takes the gin fully into the realm of the cocktail, but many famous drinkers have removed the vermouth from their favorite recipe.

"Glance at the vermouth bottle briefly while pouring the juniper distillate freely"
Winston Churchill

This style of Martini, known as arid or bone-dry, is very easy to make. Put your cocktail glass (approx. 6oz/180ml) in the freezer. Stir 2½oz (75ml) of your favorite gin over ice until it has been diluted with 1oz (30ml) of water, strain into the chilled glass, and garnish with an olive, onion, or pretty much anything you fancy.

Absinthe

The green fairy has a fearsome reputation among drinkers, with claims for hallucinogenic status and for driving Van Gogh to earlessness. Most of these rumors are simply that. Absinthe does contain thujone, a chemical with similar effects to THC, but in tiny amounts. During its heyday as the intoxicant of choice for the artist community in Paris, absinthe was often counterfeited, with dubious ingredients added to give it an extra kick, but the simple fact is that it is really, really strong. Really Strong! It is also delicious, with a drier edge than its lower ABV cousins pastis and anisette. There is never a need to drink absinthe neat. In fact, it is so strong that it is difficult to swallow, due to the amount of gas that evaporates on contact with the hot surfaces of your mouth. It is useful as a flammable ingredient; you will see it make an appearance in later sections of this book.

For the classic way of drinking absinthe, try the Absinthe Drip, which is a lovely, sophisticated summer drink. First chill a heavy wine glass and add to it 1½oz (45ml) of good-quality absinthe, such as La Fée Pernod or Absinthe, and place a slotted spoon on the top. Specialist spoons are available, but any perforated one will do. Place a sugar cube on the spoon and slowly drip about 1 cup (250ml) of chilled water on the cube, dissolving it and mixing with the spirit below. This will gently louche (turn opaque) and be ready to drink when the sugar is dissolved.

SHOTS

This chapter contains some of the most famous names in the cocktail world. Many rely on layering ingredients for visual and taste effect, which is best illustrated by the Pousse-Café. Each layer was orginally sipped carefully, so that the different spirits could be enjoyed separately. The remaining drinks in this chapter dispense with that nonsense and are designed to be downed in one.

Pousse-Café

This Pousse-Café (coffee pusher) has seven layers and is a great drink for practicing your layering skills. The number of flavors means that it tastes a bit confusing.

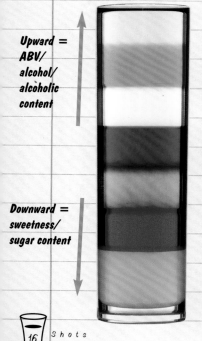

Upward = ABV/ alcohol/ alcoholic content

Downward = sweetness/ sugar content

The skill in layering a cocktail is all about being able to pour slowly and knowing where a particular spirit will rest easily on another. There is a simple rule: the sweeter an ingredient, the lower it will sit; the stronger the spirit, the higher it will sit. If in doubt, make a practice version first.

Pouring slowly can be achieved with a steady hand, but is made easier using either the pour spout of a bottle or a small pitcher. For difficult ingredients, the bar spoon comes in very handy. Set the circular base onto the layer already poured and gently pour the next spirit down the twisted stem; the liquid will then float nicely. A teaspoon will do a similar job. Simply place it, bowl up, on the top of the base layer and dribble the next ingredient into it. The illustrated drink is a proprietary secret. See if you can work out your own seven-layer Pousse-Café!

OUCH!

BRAIN HEMORRHAGE

Sounds disgusting, tastes delicious, just like a peaches and cream desert! Brain Hemorrhages are some of the easiest shots to layer, not only because the Baileys will sit on the schnapps quite easily but also because the grenadine is supposed to mix the two a little, so it doesn't really matter if the margin between them starts out a bit messy.

1 part peach schnapps
½ part Baileys
¼ part grenadine

Pour the peach schnapps into the glass, then layer the Baileys on top. Gently drop the grenadine through both layers. This should mix the two slightly, making a gross-looking swirled confection.

Squashed Frog

This is very similar to the Brain Hemorrhage but with the peach schnapps replaced by a melon liqueur. The liqueur and grenadine will mix slightly but DO NOT curdle the Baileys. There is another shot, the Cement Mixer, that uses lime cordial to do exactly that. On the premise that you should drink with friends, and I wouldn't give that to my worst enemy, I have not listed it here.

1 part Midori melon liqueur
½ part Baileys
¼ part grenadine

Pour the melon liqueur into the glass, then layer the Baileys on top. Gently drop the grenadine through both layers.

FLAT LINER

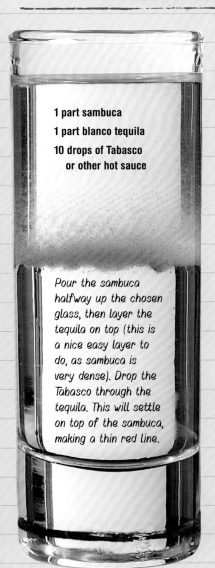

1 part sambuca

1 part blanco tequila

10 drops of Tabasco or other hot sauce

Pour the sambuca halfway up the chosen glass, then layer the tequila on top (this is a nice easy layer to do, as sambuca is very dense). Drop the Tabasco through the tequila. This will settle on top of the sambuca, making a thin red line.

One of the easiest layered shots to make and one that gets the greatest level of scared anticipation from the drinkers. It is actually not as bad as it sounds. The sweet sambuca stops the Tabasco from sticking to the mouth, so it doesn't cause long-term discomfort. If you really love spicy heat, try using a habanero-based chili sauce instead.

HOT!

Cajun
Thunder

For those people who love spice, ten drops of Tabasco in a Flat Liner (see page 19) is never going to be enough. The recipe for them is a Cajun Thunder. Taking advantage of two pieces of chemistry, it allows you to drink way more chili. Capsaicin, the active ingredient in chili, is not water-soluble, which means your saliva can't wash it away and the heat lasts for ages. It is, however, soluble in ethanol from the alcohol so stays in the mouth for less time. Sugar binds to the same receptors in the mouth, which also helps to stop much of the burning feeling.

Southern Comfort
1–100 drops of Tabasco

Pour everyone a glass of Southern Comfort. Pass around the Tabasco for people to dose their drinks. If there is more than one male in the group, this will immediately turn into a competition, with hilarious effect.

A.W.O.L

Be careful with this delicious but dangerous layered shot. If you have too many, your sanity may well go Absent Without Leave! A.W.O.L. is generally consumed while on fire but tastes just as good unlit, which is much safer. ONLY do this early on in the evening!

1 part Midori melon liqueur
1 part chilled pineapple juice
1 part vodka
½ part overproof spirit

Layer the ingredients in the order listed. The pineapple juice will layer better if well chilled. Any overproof ingredient will work for this drink but an overproof rum like Wray and Nephew or Bacardi 151 will probably taste the best.

SILENT BUT DEADLY

This is a slightly more complicated shot, which really requires someone to administer it. The premise is that breathing in the hot alcoholic vapors after the shot will speed the effect, and it might also make you sneeze.

1 part Jägermeister
½ part green Chartreuse

Pour the Jägermeister into a shot glass and float a little of the Chartreuse on top. Place the glass on a plate and pour the rest of the Chartreuse around the glass. CAREFULLY ignite everything. Hold a pint glass above the burning shot and keep there till the insides go cloudy. Extinguish by putting the pint glass down. Hold in the vapors with a napkin and drink the shot. Breathe in the vapors deeply from the pint glass.

Loretto Buzz

This is one of my favorite shots, created for Maker's Mark, who wanted a classy shot that incorporated their bourbon. The drink will also work well with other whiskey, and even with good aged rum, but Maker's has the best flavor for it.

½ part Grand Marnier
1 part champagne
½ part Maker's Mark

Layer the ingredients in a glass in the order listed. Floating the Maker's on the champagne is easier than it sounds; just make sure the champagne is well chilled. You can, of course, use any good sparkling wine for this drink, but make sure it is a brut (dry) version.

B-52

As for many modern classic cocktails, the origin of the B-52 is disputed, with many bartenders claiming to have invented it. Most attribute its name to the band rather than to the aircraft, which I believe to be wrong. The similarity of a line of B-52s being downed is a lot like carpet bombing, both in appearance and effect.

1 part Kahlua
1 part Baileys
1 part Grand Marnier

Layer the first two ingredients. Kahlua is very sweet, so the Baileys will form a layer on it with little effort. Grand Marnier is a 40% ABV (80 proof) spirit but also contains sugar, which makes layering very difficult and not helped by the bottle shape. The best way is to transfer the Grand Marnier to a small pitcher and pour VERY slowly into the bowl of a spoon resting on the Baileys.

B-55

There are many variations of the B-52, all utilizing Kahlua and Baileys as the first two layers. The drink works well with vodka, Frangelico (B-51), amaretto (B-53), and, my favorite, absinthe (B-55). The anise flavor of the absinthe adds complexity to a drink that, unlike some shots, already stands tall as a recipe with real taste merit. Due to its high alcohol content, absinthe also layers much more easily than Grand Marnier, a major consideration when you have to make ten.

1 part Kahlua
1 part Baileys
½ part absinthe

Build exactly as you would a B-52. The proportion of absinthe is lower so that the drink isn't too strong.

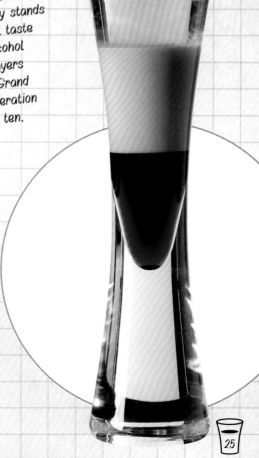

Pepino's Gun

The tequila, salt, and lime ritual is a not very nice way of hiding the taste of cheap tequila. In a perfect world, we would only drink good tequila but often people bring terrible stuff to parties. If you fancy something tasty with cheap tequila, you should try this shot. The Tajín-dipped cucumber is spicy and refreshing at the same time.

1 part tequila
1 slice of cucumber
Tajín

Tajín is a Mexican fruit seasoning made from chiles marinated in lime juice, which are then dried in the sun and ground up with rock salt. It makes a delicious rim for margaritas and also tastes great on corn on the cob. Dip the cucumber slice in the Tajín and eat after drinking the tequila. You can easily make your own version of Tajín with fresh chilies. Leave them to soak in fresh lime juice, then dry them in the oven, mix with sea salt, and grind with a pepper grinder.

BAZOOKA JOE

This is a very pretty and tasty layered shot, named after the famous comic-strip character featured inside the wrappers of Bazooka bubblegum. The ingredients are not too alcoholic and they layer very easily, while the taste is not entirely unlike bubblegum. If you can find it, bubblegum syrup makes an interesting addition to the drink.

Layer the ingredients in the order listed but be a little careful with the first layer, as different brands of curaçao and banana liqueur have different densities. You may need to switch their order around, so make a small practice drink to start with.

1 part banana liqueur
1 part blue curaçao
1 part Baileys

BOILERMAKER

The Boilermaker is the easiest drink in this book to make. It is simply a shot of whiskey with a beer on the side. There are three ways to drink a Boilermaker. The first is shooting the whiskey with the beer as a chaser; the second involves dropping the shot into the beer in the manner of a bomb, then either stirring it in or leaving it to produce a stronger drink at the end; and the third way is to tip the shot into a bottle that has had the first sip taken out of it. All three ways depend on a good pairing of whiskey and beer. I recommend a soft bourbon and a full-bodied IPA.

A light Mexican beer with a shot of tequila also makes a great Boilermaker, and one of the classic drinks of Jamaica, the Steel Bottom, involves adding a shot of Wray and Nephew overproof rum to a bottle of Red Stripe. Delicious, if deadly!

2 parts American whiskey
1 bottle of pale ale

Pickleback

Some shots sound delicious and taste horrible; some sound horrible and taste delicious. The Pickleback is one of the latter. It is simply a shot of Jameson's Irish whiskey, followed by a shot of pickle brine. The two ingredients work well together, with the warm honey notes of the whiskey complemented by the salty, sweet-and-sour finish.

Pour the two liquids into separate glasses.
Drink the whiskey, then the pickle brine. Simple.
A slice of pickle makes an excellent third stage
to the ritual. Other spirits can also be used,
including some light blended Scotch whiskies.

**1 part Jameson's
Irish whiskey**

1 part pickle brine

Flaming
BLUE LAMBORGHINI

Warning! Danger! The flaming Blue Lamborghini is a very strong drink that is also on fire! Traditionally, it is drunk while still flaming through a straw although, as you can see from the photo, that could be foolish. If you decide to try it that way, then make sure you have a long metal straw, as plastic ones will melt. To make the drink even harder to finish, it is often served with a shot of Baileys poured in at the last moment.

1 part blue curaçao

1 part vodka

1 part overproof spirit
    (absinthe works well)

1 part Baileys (optional)

Layer the top three ingredients in a small cocktail glass and carefully ignite. Either extinguish the flame or carefully drink from the bottom through a metal straw. If adding Baileys, wait until the person drinking has nearly finished before pouring it in. A Flaming Ferrari is the same drink but with a strawberry liqueur replacing the blue curaçao.

American Beauty

At first glance, this drink looks similar to a Flat Liner (see page 19), but looks can be deceiving. It is actually one of the nicest shots ever created. Named after the movie, the drink references the bed of rose petals that features heavily in the movie and also in its advertising.

- **1 part white crème de cacao**
- **1 part Stolichnaya raspberry vodka**
- **10 drops of raspberry purée**

Pour the white crème de cacao, which is colorless, in the glass, then layer the vodka on top. Drip raspberry purée through the vodka. If you are gentle, the drips will flatten out on top of the liqueur and look very much like rose petals. You can buy raspberry purée or coulis from most supermarkets but it is easy to make at home by forcing raspberries through a fine strainer.

SLIPPERY NIPPLE

This is one of the true classics of the shooter world, not only because of its name but also because the anise in the sambuca marries very well with the Irish cream liqueur. You can put a cherry at the bottom of the glass but be careful; it is possible to choke on it if you drink with too much brio.

1 part sambuca
1 part Baileys

Float the Baileys on top of the sambuca; this is a very simple float to make and doesn't require a spoon. If you want to add a cherry, place it in the glass first.

A delicious and cute shot that tastes nothing like Guinness, which for most people is a good thing. But if you do like Guinness, then head to page 62 to check out the Centurion Challenge, which could well satisfy your love of the "black stuff."

1 part Chambord raspberry liqueur

½ part Kahlua

½ part Baileys

Mix the Chambord and Kahlua together and pour into a shot glass. Float the Baileys on the top. Chambord deserves a spot in anyone's liquor cabinet but this drink also tastes really good with a crème de cassis instead.

Peanut Butter and Jelly

One of the world's all-time favorite snacks gets the shot treatment. You can shake this drink to make a uniform colored shot, but who mixes the peanut butter and jelly together before making the sandwich? The layering is the key to success (and getting right to the edges of the bread).

⅔ part Chambord raspberry liqueur

⅓ part Frangelico hazelnut liqueur

1 part Baileys

Mix the Chambord and Frangelico together, then float the Baileys on the top; this may mix slightly but don't worry. Feel free to use cassis (blackcurrant) or fraise (strawberry) liqueur instead of raspberry.

Brandy Basketball

This drink is very popular all over Southern Europe, where they love basketball. It is quite a complex ritual and requires flaming, so be careful. You can use small brandy balloons but I prefer a more hardwearing shot glass.

Dip half the orange slice in the cinnamon powder and put to one side. Carefully ignite the brandy and allow to burn for 10 seconds. Extinguish the flame by pressing your palm over the rim of the glass. The resultant vacuum will stick the glass to your hand. Impress people by mimicking a basketball dribble, shaking up the brandy. Drink in one go and bite into the cinnamon-dusted orange.

1 part cognac
1 orange slice
Cinnamon powder

BORN TO RUN

Named after "The Boss" Bruce Springsteen's seminal record, this layered shot can easily be renamed because the colors in it form the basis of a surprising number of national flags, including the UK, Russia, and Australia as well as the USA. You can buy cranberry vodka, which is red, but it's sometimes hard to get hold of. Much easier is to add a few drops of red food coloring to regular vodka.

1 part blue curaçao

1 part white crème de cacao

1 part red-colored vodka

Float all the ingredients in the order listed; the drink will taste better if they are all chilled first. Once you see how easy it is to color spirits for a particular visual effect, it will become a key skill in your shooter arsenal.

BLACK DEATH

Scarier in appearance and name than on the palate, this shot relies on Blavod, a black vodka, which is widely available and not expensive. However, you can easily re-create the effect with some black food coloring. This is easy to find at Halloween but large grocery stores will stock it year-round.

1 part sambuca

1 part Blavod black vodka

Layer the ingredients in the glass. The drink will taste better if both spirits are chilled before pouring. You can make a neat inversion of this drink with black sambuca and regular vodka. Black sambuca tastes similar to the clear version. Both are made from elderberries but in black sambuca the color of the fruit is left in the spirit.

IRISH FLAG

For a small nation, Ireland certainly punches above its weight in terms of shot and shooter ingredients. This drink uses two of the finest but, unfortunately, they don't make any green ones, so I have had to use crème de menthe for the last part of the flag. The mint flavor can get a bit overpowering, so it's best mixed with some triple sec first.

Layer the ingredients in the order listed. If you don't have any triple sec, just reduce the quantity of crème de menthe slightly and up the other ingredients, to maintain the balance of flavor.

1 part green crème de menthe/triple sec mix

1 part Baileys

1 part Jameson's Irish whiskey

GODFATHER'S BAMBINO

The Godfather is one of the great stirred cocktails, normally served on the rocks, but it can be a heavyweight choice. This small version packs the same flavor in a shot package. Just don't get mown down by too many of these smooth criminals.

1 part blended Scotch whisky

1 part amaretto

Stir the two ingredients together and pour into a shot glass. Make sure you meet the eyes of your fellow drinkers! There are many variations of The Godfather, replacing the Scotch whisky with either cognac or bourbon being two of them.

TEQUILA SLAMMER

The Tequila Slammer is a great ritual-based drink that is perfect for celebrations. You can make it with any carbonated beverage; in Mexico, it is known as a Muppet and made with sparkling grapefruit. The best version uses champagne, though, because it tastes great and the amount of bubbles produced will always catch out the unwary.

1 part blanco tequila

1 part champagne

Pour both ingredients into a small tumbler. The drinker places one hand over the glass and "slams" it onto the table. This causes the contents to froth wildly, which must be drunk before they spill. The "slam" can get quite powerful after a couple of rounds, so make sure you use tempered glasses.

Sambuca Con Mosca

Sambuca doesn't really fit in this book because to serve it straight requires no effort from the host. But at a great party you don't want to be constantly slaving away making drinks for people. Therefore, Sambuca is A Good Thing. Traditionally drunk as a digestif or with coffee, it is an acquired taste, but one that is worth acquiring. Con Mosca (With Flies) refers to serving with three coffee beans on the surface, representing health, wealth, and happiness. When serving Con Mosca, the drink is often set alight, which slightly roasts the coffee beans for a pleasing aroma. As always, be careful of letting things burn for too long, as the rim of the glass can get really hot. It is worth allowing it to cool for 30 seconds after extinguishing.

SHOOTERS

Shooter describes a cocktail that includes nonalcoholic ingredients and is shaken before serving. Shaking with ice dilutes the drinks, as well as mixing and chilling them, which means they are lower in alcoholic content than regular shots, making them great party drinks. If you are making loads of shooters, it is worth buying a large cocktail shaker, to allow you to make whole rounds in one go. Just remember that you can never have enough ice, so make sure your freezer is fully stocked.

MAPLE SLAPSHOT

Canadians are great at five things, three of them being hockey. The fourth is maple syrup, the fifth I will leave to your imagination (your author is Canadian...). It's difficult to make drinks from hockey but not from maple syrup. It is a perfect complement to the maple wood used in the production of Jack Daniel's Tennessee whiskey, so I have put these natural bedfellows together.

1¼ parts Jack Daniel's
½ part fresh lemon juice
¼ part maple syrup

Shake all the ingredients together with ice and strain into a shot glass. Maple syrup comes in different grades, referring to the strength of flavor. Try to find grade 1, as it is the lightest and will not overwhelm the whiskey.

Sherbet

This is one of my all-time favorite simple shooters. It is popular with everyone, gentle in alcohol, uses easy-to-find ingredients, and goes down an absolute treat. Using popping candy to rim the glass makes the drink a true taste sensation.

1 part Rose's Lime Cordial
Popping candy (optional)
1 part Southern Comfort

Rim the shot glass by moistening with a bit of lime cordial, then dip into a tray of the popping candy. This can be done in advance to speed up the making of the drinks. Shake the Southern Comfort and lime cordial hard with the ice and strain into the glass.

Cherry Bomb

There are lots of different cherry liqueurs on the market, and a lot of them, like Cherry Heering, include a maceration of the stones for a nutty flavor. They are delicious ingredients but for this drink you need something simpler. Most products labeled "Cherry Brandy" from producers like De Kuyper or Bols will do the trick.

½ part vodka
½ part cherry brandy
1 part champagne

Shake the vodka and cherry brandy with ice and strain into a large shot glass. Top with the champagne. This drink will also work with other sparkling wines, like prosecco. Serve with a bowl of ripe pitted cherries.

CRACKBABY

Over the last ten years, the Crackbaby has taken London by storm, becoming the most popular shooter. It is the signature drink of Boujis, the favorite nightspot of certain members of the Royal Family, where every customer will have at least one through the evening. Loosely based on the Pornstar Martini, it makes a great sidekick to a glass of champagne.

½ part vanilla vodka
½ part passionfruit juice
½ part strawberry purée
1 part champagne

Shake the first three ingredients and strain into a large shot glass, top with the champagne, and down in one. If you can't find vanilla vodka, either infuse your own or just use normal vodka; it is just as nice.

Baby Bellini

Invented in Harry's Bar in Venice, the Bellini is a fantastic blend of white peach purée and prosecco. This version has all of the great taste in a small package. Due to the low level of alcohol, these are ideal early evening shots, but if you fancy a bit more of a kick, feel free to add a dash of vodka or even brandy.

½ part peach purée
1½ parts prosecco

Stir the prosecco into the purée slowly to keep the fizz. Pour gently into a shot glass and serve. You can buy fruit purée or make your own by blending fruit and then pushing through a strainer. Using strawberry purée instead makes a Rossini. Raspberry and mango are also delicious.

LEMON DROP

If you like your drinks sharp and refreshing, this is the one for you. The key to this drink and any others requiring lime or lemon juice is to squeeze it yourself; the packaged versions are really bitter and unpleasant. A neutral Scandinavian vodka is perfect here but citrus vodka and even gin are good alternatives.

Shake the vodka and lemon juice together with ice and strain into a shot glass. Serve with a slice of lemon, sprinkled with sugar. Down the shot and then suck on the sugar-coated lemon. If you have a sweet tooth, add a little sugar to the mix before shaking.

1 part vodka
½ part fresh lemon juice
1 slice of lemon
Granulated sugar

TEQUILA ESPRESSO & VODKA ESPRESSO

So nice it's in twice! There is nothing that gets a party started like a delicious blend of alcohol and caffeine. Both of these drinks make an excellent alternative to a dessert or an energy drink. Homemade espresso is great but most machines struggle to make lots of good espresso quickly. You can, however, buy it from the local coffee shop in advance; the espresso will be fine for four hours and still make a lovely crema.

1 part tequila or vodka

½ part coffee liqueur

½ part ristretto (strong) espresso

Shake all the ingredients really hard with ice and strain into a shot glass. You can tell if you have done it correctly if it settles slowly like a Guinness. If you normally drink your coffee sweet, you can add a bit of sugar to the recipe before shaking.

Kamikaze

The Kamikaze is almost a small version of a Margarita or a Sidecar, and you can make it with practically any spirit. The classic recipe uses vodka, but flavored vodka, tequila, brandy, or rum will all be delicious.

1 part vodka

1 part triple sec or Cointreau

1 part lime juice

Shake all the ingredients hard with ice and strain into a shot glass. Down the hatch!

King Coconut Kamikaze

Rum, Coconut, and Pineapple are a marriage (threesome?) made in heaven. There are a couple of ways of making this drink. The easiest uses coconut rum, with Koko Kanu being my favorite. If you love, really love, coconut, you can buy coconut water from good grocers, which makes a delicious and slightly less sweet version.

1 part coconut rum

½ part pineapple juice

½ part lime juice

Shake all the ingredients hard with ice and strain into a shot glass. If you want to use coconut water, replace the coconut rum with regular white rum and add ½ part coconut water.

Key Lime Pie

Everyone's favorite dessert made into a delicious shot. What's not to love? Cream and citrus are difficult ingredients to use in cocktails together, as they tend to curdle. The easiest way is to use a lime vodka (Finlandia make an excellent one, although there are others). In this recipe, it's paired with limoncello, a liqueur made from macerated lemons, for a citrus bite.

1 part lime vodka
1 part limoncello
½ part heavy (double) cream

Shake the first two ingredients together and strain into a shot glass. Float the heavy cream on the top. You can use light (single) cream for a less calorific drink but you will have to whip it first. A touch of Midori melon liqueur will give the perfect Key Lime Pie color.

Pink Pussycat

This drink is as lovely as it sounds, and don't worry, it has no claws. Strawberries and cream are one of those perfect combinations, and crème de fraise is a very useful ingredient for your liquor cabinet. If you fancy a change, though, you can replace the strawberry flavor with raspberry, using Chambord or another raspberry liqueur.

Shake all the ingredients together with ice and strain into a chilled shot glass. If you can't find strawberry purée, use a little melted strawberry ice cream to replace both the purée and cream, which will give you an even richer shooter.

1 part vodka
⅓ part crème de fraise
⅓ part strawberry purée
⅓ part light (single) cream

English Rose

Roses make lovely perfume but some terrible drinks. Here, I have substituted rose for another flower, but one that makes delicious drinks: elderflower. Elderflower cordial brings a lovely, light, summery note to this shooter, and there's also some cucumber shaken in for a clean, fresh finish. Both flavors match up well with Hendrick's gin, which is infused with roses but we forgive them.

1 part Hendrick's gin
½ part elderflower cordial
½ part fresh lemon juice
1 slice of cucumber

Shake all the ingredients together with ice. If you shake hard enough, the cucumber will break apart, releasing its juice. Strain into a shot glass. For added crunch, serve with another slice of cucumber.

JUNE BUG

The June bug is a pretty creepy-looking scarab beetle but, rest assured, there are no similarities between the insect and the drink, apart from the green color. This awesome shooter also makes a great long drink—simply multiply the ingredients by four and serve over ice in a highball glass with a pineapple leaf as garnish.

1 part coconut rum
1 part Midori melon liqueur
1 part pineapple juice
Squeeze of fresh lime

Shake all the ingredients together with ice and strain into a large shot glass. If made properly, the drink will have a nice frothy head.

PARADISE PUNCH

Imagine you are on a desert island, with the sea lapping against the shore, coconut palms swaying gently in the breeze... It's an idyllic image, for about five seconds, when you realize there is no swim-up bar, no sound system, and no friends to share this delicious tropical shot with you. A delicious blend of exotic juices, it is truly a taste of paradise.

Make a mix of your favorite tropical juices; guava, pineapple, mango, and passionfruit are a good start. Shake all the ingredients, apart from the grenadine, and pour into a shot glass. Drop a little grenadine into the glass and swirl until you get a perfect sunset effect.

1 part tropical juice mix

¼ part dark rum

¼ part white rum

¼ part aged rum

¼ part maraschino liqueur

¼ part lime juice

Dash of grenadine

Brooklyn Shake

Much, much cooler than the Harlem alternative, as this doesn't involve dancing like an idiot... unless you want to! Brooklyn Lager is a great beer to use in cocktails and shooters, as it is full-flavored enough to stand up to spirituous ingredients without being too heavy, but feel free to substitute here with your favorite tipple.

1 part Drambuie
½ part fresh lemon juice
1 slice of fresh ginger
Brooklyn Lager

Shake the first three ingredients hard with ice and strain into a large shot glass. Top up with the Brooklyn. One of the best things about making this drink for friends is that you get to finish the beer... if there is any left.

ALABAMA SLAMMER

Not just somewhere you really don't want to get stuck on a summer's night but also a great shooter. There are many variations to this drink but I think the classic is the best. A lot of recipes call for "Sour Mix," but this has no place in a proper liquor cabinet. Both Southern Comfort and sloe gin are sweet, so the fresh lemon juice provides the perfect balance.

1 part Southern Comfort
1 part sloe gin
1 part fresh lemon juice

Shake all the ingredients with ice and strain into a shot glass. For a slightly softer version, you can add 1 part of fresh orange juice.

English Breakfast

I would love to make a proper "Full English" shooter but cramming bacon, sausage, beans, egg, tomato, mushrooms, and hash browns into a shot glass is impossible, although it has been tried! Instead, this is a more sensible combination of two other quintessentially English ingredients: tea and marmalade. Toast is optional.

1½ parts Absolut Wild Tea Vodka

¼ part fresh lemon juice

½ part thick-cut marmalade

Mix the marmalade with a dash of hot water to thin it down a little, then shake all the ingredients with ice and strain into a shot glass. To improve appearances, you can add some thin slices of orange zest to the glass.

Chocolate Mudslide

⅔ **part vodka**

⅔ **part white crème de cacao**

⅔ **part whole milk**

½ **part chocolate sauce**

Decadent and obviously fairly calorific, the very definition of naughty but nice. This drink requires a little preparation, as most chocolate sauces are so sticky that they just stay in the bottom of the glass. The easiest way to make the sauce is to take a small amount of drinking chocolate powder and mix up a thick batch with water. The idea is that it should flow like a mud slide into your mouth as you finish the drink.

Shake together all but the chocolate sauce with ice. Pour the sauce into the glass and float the shaken mixture on top. If you fancy, dust the top with chocolate powder.

AFTER EIGHT

Named after possibly the most addictive chocolate of all time, this drink could prove nearly as moreish. You can use either white or green crème de menthe, but if you are buying the liquor especially and are not going to finish the bottle, the green is probably more useful (see Irish Flag, page 37). But if you like stingers, made with white crème de menthe, Giffard's Menthe Pastille is the original and best.

Shake all the ingredients hard with ice and strain into a glass. The harder you shake, the more air you will incorporate and the lighter and dreamier the drink will be.

1 part crème de menthe
1 part white crème de cacao
1 part Baileys
1 part light (single) cream

Russian Quaalude

Quaalude is the brand name for an hypnotic sedative called Methaqualone. Although this drink has no mind-bending ingredients, after a few you might start to see things go a little blurry. The name would obviously suggest Russian vodka but don't worry if your favorite is Polish or Swedish as that will work just fine.

1 part vodka

1 part Frangelico hazelnut liqueur

1 part amaretto

1 part Baileys

Shake all the ingredients with ice and strain into a large shot glass. Frangelico is delicious but sometimes hard to find. If you can't get your hands on any, substitute with a little extra vodka and a dash of hazelnut syrup, available from coffee shops.

TEQUILA & SANGRITA

One of Mexico's finest contributions to the cocktail world is Sangrita. With a drink as traditional and widespread as this, there are many "authentic" recipes, and it is definitely worth experimenting to find your favorite. The mix should be savory and spicy and, of course, red. Some people base theirs on tomato juice but I prefer fresh orange and pomegranate. Feel free to add extra spice, cilantro (coriander), or even tamarind to the recipe below.

3½ tbsp (50ml) fresh lime juice

1 tbsp (20g) superfine (caster) sugar

1¼ cups (300ml) fresh orange juice

7 tbsp (100ml) fresh pomegranate juice

5 tsp (20ml) Cholula hot sauce

1 small habanero chili, seeded

1 tsp salt

Blend all the ingredients together until smooth, and refrigerate. Pomegranates are easy to juice with a citrus juicer, provided they are ripe. Otherwise, use a good-quality packaged juice. Makes a pitcher.

SURFER ON ACID

Legend says the Harvey Wallbanger was named after a surfer who ordered his Screwdriver with a shot of Galliano to give it more flavor and an extra kick, and then proceeded to walk into walls. This drink is what would happen if he had gone a step further...

1 part coconut rum
½ part pineapple juice
½ part Jägermeister

Stir the first two ingredients together with ice until chilled (if you shake it, you will get too much froth). Float the Jägermeister on the top. Traditionally, this shot is consumed from the bottom with a straw, so you finish with a hit of Jäger.

BRAIN FREEZE

This drink gets half its effect from the challenge of drinking a super cold drink without getting the eponymous "Brain Freeze." You can make loads of different flavors, using your favorite fruit and matching liqueur as the sweetener. If in doubt, try watermelon and Midori, raspberry and Chambord, as well as the strawberry version below.

4 parts light rum
2 parts crème de fraise
2 strawberries
1 part fresh lemon juice

Blend all the ingredients together with ½ cup of crushed ice until smooth. Pour into four shot glasses and serve. For an even more pronounced effect, try drinking them through a straw.

Black Forest Gateau

After the Hamburger and the Frankfurter, the third most delicious food to come out of Germany is the extravagant cake from the Schwarzwald – a combination of chocolate, cherry, and kirsch. This liquid version has all the flavor and doesn't even need a spoon. Perfect!

1 part dark crème de cacao
1 part cherry brandy
1 part cognac
1 part heavy (double) cream

Shake the first three ingredients with ice and strain into a large shot glass, then float the cream on top. If you live near a patisserie, you may be able to buy edible chocolate straws, which are the perfect accompaniment.

Purple Hooter

The most usual time to see a big red nose is at the circus, on a clown. You don't need to wear massive shoes but this drink may make you act the fool... It is really simple to make, and uses Rose's Lime Cordial instead of fresh lime juice, saving time on preparation. If you are only making a couple, it is worth trying with fresh limes to see if you prefer it.

1 part vodka

⅔ part Chambord raspberry liqueur

⅓ part Rose's Lime Cordial

Shake all the ingredients with ice and strain into a shot glass. You can try this with flavored vodkas; lemon and lime work particularly well.

GAMES & RITUALS

JÄGERBOMB

Few drinks have captured the imagination, and the money, of so many people in such a short length of time as the Jägerbomb. Why? Because it completes the set of attributes required for the perfect shot. It's challenging to drink in the mind but, surprisingly, easier to do in the mouth; it incorporates interesting mouth-filling flavors and a great blend of alcohol and caffeine in the same glass; it's easy to make and has a great ritual that encourages people to get excited even before they have had the drink. I love them and am obviously not alone.

The Jägerbomb requires little explanation of method: simply drop a shot glass of Jägermeister into a half-full tumbler of Red Bull or other energy drink. How do you make it even better? If you choose your shot/tumbler combination well, you can balance the shot on the rim for great presentation, but even better is the cascade. Line up 10, 20, even 100 tumblers with their edges touching, carefully balance a shot glass on each pair of edges, and fill with Jäger. Knock over the first shot glass and watch in awe as they all topple like dominoes into the glasses, making the whole party a round of perfect Jägerbombs. Awesome.

For the three people in the world who don't like this drink, or for people looking for the new thing, why not try a Sailor Bomb? Make it in exactly the same way but using Sailor Jerry Spiced Rum and ginger beer. Delicious.

Tangled Twister

The best thing about doing shots is the way they get the party started and bring people together. If you go to an "Adults" party, they might bring out a board game to encourage further fun after the dinner is over. Here, however, I have decided to bring the two concepts of shots and games together.

Lots of lemons
Lots of vodka
Chambord raspberry liqueur
Blue curaçao
Crème de banane
Midori melon liqueur
Lots of shot glasses
Game of Twister

Juice the lemons and make up a batch of your basic shot mix using 2 parts vodka and ½ part lemon juice. Shake this up, or mix in a punch bowl, with ice. Pour into shot glasses and add ½ part of either a red, blue, yellow, or green liqueur to each glass.

Play Twister. Either as a forfeit or just as a between-rounds livener, everyone spins the wheel and drinks a shot corresponding to the color they land on. Simple. And AMAZING!

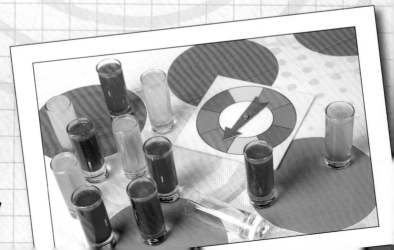

Shot Glass Chess/Checkers

The competitive spirit is alive in everyone, but some people just hide it better. This game is a great way to unleash the inner winner (or loser). Chess relies on thinking several moves ahead, on strategy rather than tactics, and a clear head. To make the game more fun, how about you replace the chess pieces with shots? This can be as simple as marking shot glasses with a symbol of the piece – indeed, you can buy shot glass chess sets that do exactly that – but I think it is worth assembling your own board from different glasses. These can be bought from flea markets, stolen from bars, etc.

Ingredients for your favorite shots

32 shot glasses

Chessboard

Mix up your favorite shot from the book. Fill the glasses and place them on the chessboard. Now let's play!

The rules are the same as competition chess, with a time limit of one minute per move. When a piece is taken, someone has to drink the contents of the glass. There are two possible options here. Either you drink the pieces you take or your pieces that are taken. Each variation produces a very different style of game.

If you're brave, or impatient, you can play checkers instead. In this game, you drink your own pieces, and if you manage to king a piece, your opponent has to drink the shot.

Be warned: checkers is a fast-paced game, so make small shots of some of the less strong drinks or you'll be in trouble.

CENTURION CHALLENGE

The Centurion Challenge is one of those peculiar exercises that sounds really easy in theory but proves near impossible in reality. The premise is very simple: drink 100 shots of beer in 100 minutes.

Set up the shot glasses with beer and start the clock. The rules are simple.

You must keep ahead of the clock; if at 59 minutes you have drunk less than 59 shots, you are out of the game.

You must drink from a shot glass. This ensures you get the maximum amount of gas from each shot.

You can drink at whatever speed you want. Just remember who won between the hare and the tortoise...

The key to a successful game is to make it hard but not impossible. A British single shot x 100 equates to 4½ pints (2.5 liters), which is achievable. An American shot equates to 5¼ pints (2.8 liters), which is borderline. Big shot glasses, however, can be 2oz (60ml). You do the math.

The winner is the first man to finish, or the last man standing. Cheers!

Drink 100 shots of beer in 100 minutes

Lots and LOTS of shot glasses (you don't need 100 each but at least 10 per person playing)

Lots of beer. It's great to offer up a range of beer to the players, because that's when strategy comes in to play. Should they choose a light lager, which is easy to drink but very fizzy, or a heavier beer, which has less gas and might also be lower in alcohol?

Russian Roulette

The multibillion dollar gambling industry demonstrates that people love a game of chance, and also that they don't mind losing. Even better than losing is watching your friends lose.

This game combines all the best aspects of a game of cards: your chance to be lucky in the face of seemingly impossible odds, the requirement to keep a poker face, and the chance to see someone go all in and get a busted flush.

Lots of vodka

Lots of water

2 identical pitchers

Lots of small shot glasses

The premise couldn't be simpler. Take loads of shot glasses and fill half with vodka and half with water from the two pitchers. Place the shots in the center of the table and take turns picking a glass and drinking the contents. If the person drinking gets water or, importantly, can convince the other players that it's water, the water is replaced by that player with a shot of vodka (they may well make a mistake at this point because they don't know which pitcher is which). If they get a shot of water, this is replaced with vodka in the same way. They can, of course, pretend that it's vodka, reversing the process.

People start to guess which pitcher is which, and try and follow the glasses to remember the positioning, but the person who has just completed the shot can mix them up.

If vodka is too high stakes, you can mix it with cranberry juice or your favorite mixer, but I guarantee that everyone at the table will have a) the time of their lives and b) a sore head in the morning.

Index